THIS PLANNER
BELONGS TO

Candi Turnu

A LITTLE GOD TIME

2017
16-MONTH
WEEKLY PLANNER

BELLE
· CITY ·
GIFTS

SEPTEMBER 2016						
S	M	T	W	T	F	S
				1	2	3
4	5	6	7	8	9	10
11	12	13	14	15	16	17
18	19	20	21	22	23	24
25	26	27	28	29	30	

OCTOBER 2016						
S	M	T	W	T	F	S
						1
2	3	4	5	6	7	8
9	10	11	12	13	14	15
16	17	18	19	20	21	22
23	24	25	26	27	28	29
30	31					

NOVEMBER 2016						
S	M	T	W	T	F	S
		1	2	3	4	5
6	7	8	9	10	11	12
13	14	15	16	17	18	19
20	21	22	23	24	25	26
27	28	29	30			

DECEMBER 2016						
S	M	T	W	T	F	S
				1	2	3
4	5	6	7	8	9	10
11	12	13	14	15	16	17
18	19	20	21	22	23	24
25	26	27	28	29	30	31

JANUARY 2017						
S	M	T	W	T	F	S
1	2	3	4	5	6	7
8	9	10	11	12	13	14
15	16	17	18	19	20	21
22	23	24	25	26	27	28
29	30	31				

FEBRUARY 2017						
S	M	T	W	T	F	S
			1	2	3	4
5	6	7	8	9	10	11
12	13	14	15	16	17	18
19	20	21	22	23	24	25
26	27	28				

MARCH 2017						
S	M	T	W	T	F	S
			1	2	3	4
5	6	7	8	9	10	11
12	13	14	15	16	17	18
19	20	21	22	23	24	25
26	27	28	29	30	31	

APRIL 2017						
S	M	T	W	T	F	S
						1
2	3	4	5	6	7	8
9	10	11	12	13	14	15
16	17	18	19	20	21	22
23	24	25	26	27	28	29
30						

MAY 2017						
S	M	T	W	T	F	S
	1	2	3	4	5	6
7	8	9	10	11	12	13
14	15	16	17	18	19	20
21	22	23	24	25	26	27
28	29	30	31			

JUNE 2017						
S	M	T	W	T	F	S
				1	2	3
4	5	6	7	8	9	10
11	12	13	14	15	16	17
18	19	20	21	22	23	24
25	26	27	28	29	30	

JULY 2017						
S	M	T	W	T	F	S
						1
2	3	4	5	6	7	8
9	10	11	12	13	14	15
16	17	18	19	20	21	22
23	24	25	26	27	28	29
30	31					

AUGUST 2017						
S	M	T	W	T	F	S
		1	2	3	4	5
6	7	8	9	10	11	12
13	14	15	16	17	18	19
20	21	22	23	24	25	26
27	28	29	30	31		

SEPTEMBER 2017						
S	M	T	W	T	F	S
					1	2
3	4	5	6	7	8	9
10	11	12	13	14	15	16
17	18	19	20	21	22	23
24	25	26	27	28	29	30

OCTOBER 2017						
S	M	T	W	T	F	S
1	2	3	4	5	6	7
8	9	10	11	12	13	14
15	16	17	18	19	20	21
22	23	24	25	26	27	28
29	30	31				

NOVEMBER 2017						
S	M	T	W	T	F	S
			1	2	3	4
5	6	7	8	9	10	11
12	13	14	15	16	17	18
19	20	21	22	23	24	25
26	27	28	29	30		

DECEMBER 2017						
S	M	T	W	T	F	S
					1	2
3	4	5	6	7	8	9
10	11	12	13	14	15	16
17	18	19	20	21	22	23
24	25	26	27	28	29	30
31						

INTRODUCTION

Having trouble fitting everything in your day? This 16-month planner makes getting organized simple and inspiring.

Each beautifully designed page blends practical weekly plans with motivating Scripture. High-quality paper allows you to confidently write reminders, schedules, and personal notes in the space provided.

Stay organized, and be refreshed and inspired as you make A Little God Time part of your day.

SEPTEMBER
2016

One thing I have desired of the LORD,

That will I seek:

That I may dwell in the house of the LORD

All the days of my life,

To behold the beauty of the LORD ,

And to inquire in His temple.

PSALM 27:4 NKJV

S	M	T	W	T	F	S
				1	2	3
4	5	6	7	8	9	10
11	12	13	14	15	16	17
18	19	20	21	22	23	24
25	26	27	28	29	30	

"Peace I leave with you; my peace I give you. I do not give to you as the world gives. Do not let your hearts be troubled and do not be afraid."

JOHN 14:27 NIV

AUGUST/SEPTEMBER

29 Monday

_____
_____
_____
_____

30 Tuesday

_____
_____
_____
_____

31 Wednesday

_____
_____
_____
_____

Thursday 1

Friday 2

Saturday 3

Sunday 4

THE LORD WILL GIVE STRENGTH TO HIS PEOPLE;
THE LORD WILL BLESS HIS PEOPLE WITH PEACE.

Psalm 29:11 NKJV

*Let perseverance finish its work
so that you may be mature
and complete, not lacking anything.*

JAMES 1:4 NIV

SEPTEMBER

5 Monday LABOR DAY

_____
_____
_____
_____

6 Tuesday

_____
_____
_____
_____

7 Wednesday

_____
_____
_____
_____

BLESSED IS ANYONE WHO ENDURES TEMPTATION.
SUCH A ONE HAS STOOD THE TEST AND WILL RECEIVE
THE CROWN OF LIFE THAT THE LORD HAS PROMISED
TO THOSE WHO LOVE HIM.

James 1:12 NRSV

Don't worry about anything;
instead, pray about everything.
Tell God what you need,
and thank him for all he has done.

PHILIPPIANS 4:6 NLT

SEPTEMBER

12 Monday

13 Tuesday

14 Wednesday

Thursday 15

Friday 16

Saturday 17

Sunday 18

My voice You shall hear in the morning, O LORD;
In the morning I will direct it to You,
And I will look up.

PSALM 5:3 NKJV

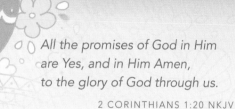

*All the promises of God in Him
are Yes, and in Him Amen,
to the glory of God through us.*

2 CORINTHIANS 1:20 NKJV

SEPTEMBER

19 Monday

_____
_____
_____
_____

20 Tuesday

_____
_____
_____
_____

21 Wednesday

_____
_____
_____
_____

_____
_____
_____
_____
_____

Friday 23

_____
_____
_____
_____

Saturday 24

_____
_____
_____

Sunday 25

_____
_____
_____

THE LORD ALWAYS KEEPS HIS PROMISES;
HE IS GRACIOUS IN ALL HE DOES.

Psalm 145:13 NLT

If you declare with your mouth, "Jesus is Lord," and believe in your heart that God raised him from the dead, you will be saved.

ROMANS 10:9 NIV

SEPTEMBER/OCTOBER

26 Monday

_____

_____

_____

_____

27 Tuesday

_____

_____

_____

_____

_____

28 Wednesday

_____

_____

_____

_____

Thursday 29

_____

_____

_____

_____

Friday 30

_____

_____

_____

_____

Saturday 1

_____

_____

ROSH HASHANAH BEGINS Sunday 2

_____

_____

_____

YOUR PROMISES HAVE BEEN THOROUGHLY TESTED,
AND YOUR SERVANT LOVES THEM.

Psalm 119:40 NIV

OCTOBER
2016

Be truly glad! There is wonderful joy

ahead.... You love him even though you

have never seen him. Though you do

not see him now, you trust him; and you

rejoice with a glorious, inexpressible joy.

1 PETER 1:6, 8–9 NLT

S	M	T	W	T	F	S
						1
2	3	4	5	6	7	8
9	10	11	12	13	14	15
16	17	18	19	20	21	22
23	24	25	26	27	28	29
30	31					

Become complete. Be of good comfort, be of one mind, live in peace; and the God of love and peace will be with you.

2 CORINTHIANS 13:11 NKJV

OCTOBER

3 Monday

_____
_____
_____
_____

4 Tuesday   ROSH HASHANAH ENDS

_____
_____
_____
_____

5 Wednesday

_____
_____
_____
_____

Thursday 6

_____

_____

_____

_____

_____

Friday 7

_____

_____

_____

_____

_____

Saturday 8

_____

_____

_____

Sunday 9

_____

_____

_____

THE DESIRES OF THE DILIGENT ARE FULLY SATISFIED.

Proverbs 13:4 NIV

The grass withers,
And its flower falls away,
But the word of the LORD
endures forever.

1 PETER 1:24-25 NKJV

OCTOBER

10 Monday COLUMBUS DAY

_____
_____
_____
_____
_____

11 Tuesday YOM KIPPUR BEGINS

_____
_____
_____
_____
_____

12 Wednesday YOM KIPPUR ENDS

_____
_____
_____
_____
_____

HE WILL GIVE ETERNAL LIFE TO THOSE WHO
KEEP ON DOING GOOD,
SEEKING AFTER THE GLORY AND HONOR AND
IMMORTALITY THAT GOD OFFERS.

Romans 2:7 NLT

Always give yourselves fully to the work of the Lord, because you know that your labor in the Lord is not in vain.

1 CORINTHIANS 15:58 NIV

OCTOBER

17 Monday

_____
_____
_____
_____

18 Tuesday

_____
_____
_____
_____

19 Wednesday

_____
_____
_____
_____

Thursday 20

_____

_____

_____

_____

Friday 21

_____

_____

_____

_____

Saturday 22

_____

_____

_____

Sunday 23

_____

_____

_____

My flesh and my heart may fail,
but God is the strength of my heart
and my portion forever.

Psalm 73:26 NIV

The LORD is my strength and my shield;
My heart trusts in him, and I am helped.

PSALM 28:7 NASB

OCTOBER

24 Monday

_____
_____
_____
_____

25 Tuesday

_____
_____
_____
_____

26 Wednesday

_____
_____
_____
_____

Thursday 27

Friday 28

Saturday 29

Sunday 30

BUT FOR YOU WHO FEAR MY NAME,
THE SUN OF RIGHTEOUSNESS SHALL RISE
WITH HEALING IN ITS WINGS.

Malachi 4:2 ESV

NOVEMBER
2016

Praise the LORD!

Praise God in his sanctuary;

praise him in his mighty heavens!

Praise him for his mighty deeds;

praise him according to his excellent greatness!

Let everything that has breath praise the LORD!

Praise the LORD!

PSALM 150:1-2, 6 ESV

S	M	T	W	T	F	S
		1	2	3	4	5
6	7	8	9	10	11	12
13	14	15	16	17	18	19
20	21	22	23	24	25	26
27	28	29	30			

Commit your actions to the LORD.
and your plans will succeed.

PROVERBS 16:3 NLT

OCTOBER/NOVEMBER

31 Monday

_____
_____
_____
_____

1 Tuesday

_____
_____
_____
_____
_____

2 Wednesday

_____
_____
_____
_____

Thursday 3

Friday 4

Saturday 5

Sunday 6

THOSE WHO KNOW YOUR NAME WILL PUT THEIR TRUST IN YOU;
FOR YOU, LORD, HAVE NOT FORSAKEN THOSE WHO SEEK YOU.

Psalm 9:10 NKJV

The LORD is for me; he will help me.
It is better to take refuge in the LORD
than to trust in people.

PSALM 118:7-8 NLT

NOVEMBER

7 Monday

8 Tuesday ELECTION DAY

9 Wednesday

Thursday 10

_____

_____

_____

_____

_____

Friday 11

_____

_____

_____

_____

_____

Saturday 12

_____

_____

_____

Sunday 13

_____

_____

_____

I TRUST IN YOU, O LORD;
I SAY, "YOU ARE MY GOD."
MY TIMES ARE IN YOUR HAND.

Psalm 31:14-15 ESV

I keep my eyes always on the LORD.
With him at my right hand,
I will not be shaken.

PSALM 16:8 NIV

NOVEMBER

14 Monday

_____
_____
_____
_____

15 Tuesday

_____
_____
_____
_____

16 Wednesday

_____
_____
_____
_____

Thursday 17

Friday 18

Saturday 19

Sunday 20

THE LAW OF THE LORD IS PERFECT,
REFRESHING THE SOUL.

Psalm 19:7 NIV

*"If you abide in My word,
you are My disciples indeed.
And you shall know the truth,
and the truth shall make you free."*

JOHN 8:31-32 NKJV

NOVEMBER

21 Monday

_____
_____
_____
_____

22 Tuesday

_____
_____
_____
_____
_____

23 Wednesday

_____
_____
_____
_____

Thursday 24

_____
_____
_____
_____
_____

Friday 25

_____
_____
_____
_____
_____

Saturday 26

_____
_____
_____

FIRST SUNDAY OF ADVENT **Sunday** 27

_____
_____
_____

YOU WERE CLEANSED FROM YOUR SINS WHEN YOU OBEYED THE TRUTH.

1 Peter 1:22 NLT

DECEMBER
2016

O Lord, You have searched me and known me.

You know my sitting down and my rising up;

You understand my thought afar off.

You comprehend my path and my lying down,

And are acquainted with all my ways.

For there is not a word on my tongue,

But behold, O Lord, You know it altogether.

PSALM 139:1-4 NKJV

S	M	T	W	T	F	S
				1	2	3
4	5	6	7	8	9	10
11	12	13	14	15	16	17
18	19	20	21	22	23	24
25	26	27	28	29	30	31

*Blessed is the one who finds wisdom,
and the one who gets understanding.*

PROVERBS 3:13 ESV

NOVEMBER/DECEMBER

28 Monday

_____
_____
_____
_____

29 Tuesday

_____
_____
_____
_____

30 Wednesday

_____
_____
_____
_____

Thursday 1

Friday 2

Saturday 3

Sunday 4

DO NOT LET WISDOM AND UNDERSTANDING OUT OF YOUR SIGHT,
PRESERVE SOUND JUDGMENT AND DISCRETION;
THEY WILL BE LIFE FOR YOU.

Proverbs 3:21-22 NIV

Oh, the depth of the riches both of the wisdom and knowledge of God! How unsearchable are His judgments and unfathomable His ways!

ROMANS 11:33 NASB

DECEMBER

5 Monday

_____

_____

_____

_____

6 Tuesday

_____

_____

_____

_____

7 Wednesday

_____

_____

_____

_____

Thursday 8

_____

_____

_____

_____

_____

Friday 9

_____

_____

_____

_____

Saturday 10

_____

_____

Sunday 11

_____

_____

_____

THE LORD GIVES WISDOM;
FROM HIS MOUTH COME KNOWLEDGE AND UNDERSTANDING.

Proverbs 2:6-7 ESV

If any of you lacks wisdom, you should ask God, who gives generously to all without finding fault, and it will be given to you.

JAMES 1:5 NIV

DECEMBER

12 Monday

_____
_____
_____
_____
_____

13 Tuesday

_____
_____
_____
_____
_____

14 Wednesday

_____
_____
_____
_____
_____

Thursday 15

_____

_____

_____

_____

Friday 16

_____

_____

_____

Saturday 17

_____

_____

_____

Sunday 18

_____

_____

_____

THE WISDOM FROM ABOVE IS FIRST OF ALL PURE.
IT IS ALSO PEACE LOVING, GENTLE AT ALL TIMES,
AND WILLING TO YIELD TO OTHERS.
IT IS FULL OF MERCY AND GOOD DEEDS.
IT SHOWS NO FAVORITISM AND IS ALWAYS SINCERE.

James 3:17 NLT

*Give your burdens to the LORD,
and he will take care of you.
He will not permit the godly
to slip and fall.*

PSALM 55:22 NLT

DECEMBER

19 Monday

20 Tuesday

21 Wednesday WINTER SOLSTICE

Thursday 22

Friday 23

Saturday 24

CHRISTMAS DAY / HANUKKAH BEGINS Sunday 25

YOU WILL EXPERIENCE GOD'S PEACE,
WHICH EXCEEDS ANYTHING WE CAN UNDERSTAND.
HIS PEACE WILL GUARD YOUR HEARTS AND MINDS
AS YOU LIVE IN CHRIST JESUS.

Philippians 4:7 NLT

Some people are like land that gets plenty of rain. The land produces a good crop for those who work it, and it receives God's blessings.

HEBREWS 6:7 NCV

DECEMBER

26 Monday

_____
_____
_____
_____

27 Tuesday

_____
_____
_____
_____
_____

28 Wednesday

_____
_____
_____
_____

Thursday 29

Friday 30

Saturday 31

Sunday 1

HE WHO HAS CLEAN HANDS AND A PURE HEART,
WHO HAS NOT LIFTED UP HIS SOUL TO FALSEHOOD
AND HAS NOT SWORN DECEITFULLY.
HE SHALL RECEIVE A BLESSING FROM THE LORD
AND RIGHTEOUSNESS FROM THE GOD OF HIS SALVATION.

Psalm 24:5 NASB

JANUARY
2017

God has said,

"I will never fail you.

I will never abandon you."

So we can say with confidence,

"The Lord is my helper,

so I will have no fear."

HEBREWS 13:5-6 NLT

S	M	T	W	T	F	S
1	2	3	4	5	6	7
8	9	10	11	12	13	14
15	16	17	18	19	20	21
22	23	24	25	26	27	28
29	30	31				

The Lord himself goes before you and will be with you; he will never leave you nor forsake you.

DEUTERONOMY 31:8 NIV

JANUARY

2 Monday

_____
_____
_____
_____

3 Tuesday

_____
_____
_____
_____
_____

4 Wednesday

_____
_____
_____
_____

_____

_____

_____

_____

_____

_____

_____

_____

_____

_____

_____

_____

_____

_____

THE LORD LOVES JUSTICE AND FAIRNESS;
HE WILL NEVER ABANDON HIS PEOPLE.
THEY WILL BE KEPT SAFE FOREVER.

Psalm 37:28 TLB

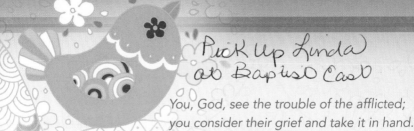

Pick Up Linda
at Baptist East

You, God, see the trouble of the afflicted;
you consider their grief and take it in hand.
The victims commit themselves to you;
you are the helper of the fatherless.

PSALM 10:14 NIV

JANUARY

9 Monday   Kristeen - salvation
            Rachael -

Linda Path - Thursday Precious
10 Tuesday
    Brenda
    Jason - Curriculum

    Bobbie Craddy
    Ronald & Jacob
11 Wednesday
    Ronnas nephews & nieces   Paul Carruth
    Rusty wife - cancer   Kra
    Samatha
    Linda B - salvation

Janie Purvis

Kellys family

Lindas son- Kyan test

Susan - Diabetics

Robbie Eye Sight - Glaucoma

Peggy Grandson

Ronnies Hip

Linda Pate - heart ablation lungs 55%

Betti Owens - Jeff

Sherry- Janies husband's sister

Mellotts family

Jeanne + Candy cleaning

Aubrey

Barbaras health - Feb. 9

Linda Burk -

Aubrey

THE LORD HEARS HIS PEOPLE WHEN THEY CALL TO HIM FOR HELP.
HE RESCUES THEM FROM ALL THEIR TROUBLES.

Psalm 34:17 NLT

The LORD does not see as man sees;
for man looks at the outward appearance,
but the LORD looks at the heart.

1 SAMUEL 16:7 NKJV

JANUARY

16 **Monday** MARTIN LUTHER KING DAY

17 Tuesday

18 Wednesday

Thursday 19

_____
_____
_____
_____
_____

Friday 20

_____
_____
_____
_____
_____

Saturday 21

_____
_____
_____

Sunday 22

_____
_____
_____

IF GOD IS FOR US, WHO CAN BE AGAINST US?

Romans 8:31 ESV

It was for freedom that Christ set us free; therefore keep standing firm and do not be subject again to a yoke of slavery.

GALATIANS 5:1 NASB

JANUARY

23 Monday

_____

_____

_____

_____

24 Tuesday

_____

_____

_____

_____

25 Wednesday

_____

_____

_____

_____

Thursday 26

Friday 27

Saturday 28

Sunday 29

Submit to God. Resist the devil and he will flee from you.

James 4:7 NKJV

FEBRUARY
2017

Take delight in the Lord,

and he will give you your heart's desires.

Commit everything you do to the Lord.

Trust him, and he will help you.

PSALM 37:4-5 NLT

S	M	T	W	T	F	S
			1	2	3	4
5	6	7	8	9	10	11
12	13	14	15	16	17	18
19	20	21	22	23	24	25
26	27	28				

Everyone should be quick to listen, slow to speak and slow to become angry, because human anger does not produce the righteousness that God desires.

JAMES 1:19-20 NIV

JANUARY/FEBRUARY

30 Monday

31 Tuesday

1 Wednesday

_____

_____

_____

_____

_____

Friday 3

_____

_____

_____

_____

Saturday 4

_____

_____

_____

Sunday 5

_____

_____

_____

THOSE WITH GOOD SENSE ARE SLOW TO ANGER,
AND IT IS THEIR GLORY TO OVERLOOK AN OFFENSE.

Proverbs 19:11 NRSV

*Cast all your anxiety on him,
because he cares for you.*

1 PETER 5:7 NRSV

FEBRUARY

6 Monday

_____
_____
_____
_____

7 Tuesday

_____
_____
_____
_____

8 Wednesday

_____
_____
_____
_____

Jon Gotti
Jenn Auguste
Mark Allen Patton > Haiti

YOU KEEP HIM IN PERFECT PEACE
WHOSE MIND IS STAYED ON YOU,
BECAUSE HE TRUSTS IN YOU.

Isaiah 26:3 ESV

To all who did accept him and believe in him he gave the right to become children of God.

JOHN 1:12 NCV

FEBRUARY

13 Monday

14 Tuesday   VALENTINE'S DAY

15 Wednesday

Thursday 16

_____
_____
_____
_____

Friday 17

_____
_____
_____
_____

Saturday 18

_____
_____

Sunday 19

_____
_____
_____

"BLESSED ARE THOSE WHO HAVE NOT SEEN AND YET HAVE BELIEVED."

John 20:29 ESV

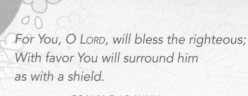

For You, O L<small>ORD</small>, will bless the righteous;
With favor You will surround him
as with a shield.

PSALM 5:12 NKJV

FEBRUARY

20 Monday   PRESIDENTS' DAY

_____
_____
_____
_____
_____

21 Tuesday

_____
_____
_____
_____
_____

22 Wednesday

_____
_____
_____
_____
_____

Friday 24

Peggy Grandson / Paul, prison

Saturday 25

Sunday 26

SURELY YOU HAVE GRANTED HIM UNENDING BLESSINGS
AND MADE HIM GLAD WITH THE JOY OF YOUR PRESENCE.

Psalm 21:6 NIV

Do not merely look out for your own personal interests, but also for the interests of others.

PHILIPPIANS 2:4 NASB

FEBRUARY/MARCH

27 Monday

28 Tuesday

1 Wednesday ASH WEDNESDAY

Thursday 2

_____

_____

_____

_____

Friday 3

_____

_____

_____

_____

Saturday 4

_____

_____

Sunday 5

_____

_____

_____

RELIGION THAT IS PURE AND UNDEFILED BEFORE GOD,
THE FATHER, IS THIS: TO CARE FOR ORPHANS AND WIDOWS IN
THEIR DISTRESS, AND TO KEEP ONESELF UNSTAINED BY THE WORLD.

James 1:27 NRSV

MARCH
2017

Blessed be the God and Father of our Lord Jesus Christ, who has blessed us in Christ with every spiritual blessing in the heavenly places, even as he chose us in him before the foundation of the world, that we should be holy and blameless before him.

EPHESIANS 1:3-4 ESV

S	M	T	W	T	F	S
			1	2	3	4
5	6	7	8	9	10	11
12	13	14	15	16	17	18
19	20	21	22	23	24	25
26	27	28	29	30	31	

*Jesus Christ is the same yesterday
and today and forever.*

HEBREWS 13:8 NASB

MARCH

6 Monday

_____
_____
_____
_____

7 Tuesday

_____
_____
_____
_____

8 Wednesday

_____
_____
_____
_____

Thursday 9

_____

_____

_____

_____

Friday 10

_____

_____

_____

_____

Saturday 11

_____

_____

_____

DAYLIGHT SAVING TIME BEGINS Sunday 12

_____

_____

_____

EVERY GOOD GIFT AND EVERY PERFECT GIFT IS FROM ABOVE,
COMING DOWN FROM THE FATHER OF LIGHTS WITH WHOM THERE
IS NO VARIATION OR SHADOW DUE TO CHANGE.

James 1:17 ESV

*Commit your work to the LORD,
and your plans will be established.*

PROVERBS 16:3 ESV

MARCH

13 Monday

_____
_____
_____
_____

14 Tuesday

_____
_____
_____
_____

15 Wednesday

_____
_____
_____
_____

Adam - Please
Margaret - Better
~~Reggie~~ - Better
Karen Elizabeth
Rosalyn = ;

Peggy Lupan

"SEEK FIRST THE KINGDOM OF GOD AND HIS RIGHTEOUSNESS,
AND ALL THESE THINGS SHALL BE ADDED TO YOU."

Matthew 6:33 NKJV

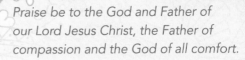

Praise be to the God and Father of our Lord Jesus Christ, the Father of compassion and the God of all comfort.

2 CORINTHIANS 1:3 NIV

MARCH

20 Monday SPRING EQUINOX

_____
_____
_____
_____
_____

21 Tuesday

_____
_____
_____
_____
_____

22 Wednesday

_____
_____
_____
_____
_____

Thursday 23

_____

_____

_____

_____

_____

Friday 24

_____

_____

_____

_____

_____

Saturday 25

_____

_____

_____

Sunday 26

_____

_____

_____

YET THE LORD LONGS TO BE GRACIOUS TO YOU;
THEREFORE HE WILL RISE UP TO SHOW YOU COMPASSION.
FOR THE LORD IS A GOD OF JUSTICE.
BLESSED ARE ALL WHO WAIT FOR HIM!

Isaiah 30:18 NIV

I am confident of this very thing, that He who began a good work in you will perfect it until the day of Christ Jesus.

PHILIPPIANS 1:6 NASB

MARCH/APRIL

27 Monday

_____
_____
_____
_____

28 Tuesday

_____
_____
_____
_____
_____

29 Wednesday

_____
_____
_____
_____
_____

Thursday 30

_____

_____

_____

_____

_____

Friday 31

_____

_____

_____

_____

_____

Saturday 1

_____

_____

_____

Sunday 2

_____

_____

_____

I CAN DO EVERYTHING THROUGH CHRIST, WHO GIVES ME STRENGTH.

Philippians 4:13 NLT

APRIL
2017

I will sing of the Lord's great love forever;

with my mouth I will make your faithfulness

known through all generations.

I will declare that your

love stands firm forever,

that you have established

your faithfulness in heaven itself.

PSALM 89:1-2 NIV

S	M	T	W	T	F	S
						1
2	3	4	5	6	7	8
9	10	11	12	13	14	15
16	17	18	19	20	21	22
23	24	25	26	27	28	29
30						

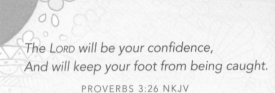

The LORD will be your confidence,
And will keep your foot from being caught.

PROVERBS 3:26 NKJV

APRIL

3   Monday

_____
_____
_____
_____

4   Tuesday

_____
_____
_____
_____

5   Wednesday

_____
_____
_____
_____

Thursday 6

_____

_____

_____

_____

_____

Friday 7

_____

_____

_____

_____

Saturday 8

_____

_____

_____

PALM SUNDAY Sunday 9

_____

_____

_____

LET US THEN APPROACH GOD'S THRONE OF GRACE
WITH CONFIDENCE, SO THAT WE MAY RECEIVE MERCY
AND FIND GRACE TO HELP US IN OUR TIME OF NEED.

Hebrews 4:16 NIV

This is the confidence that we have toward him, that if we ask anything according to his will he hears us. And if we know that he hears us in whatever we ask, we know that we have the requests that we have asked of him.

1 JOHN 5:14 ESV

APRIL

10 Monday

_____
_____
_____
_____

11 Tuesday   FIRST DAY OF PASSOVER

_____
_____
_____
_____

12 Wednesday

_____
_____
_____
_____

Thursday 13

_____

_____

_____

_____

_____

GOOD FRIDAY Friday 14

_____

_____

_____

_____

Saturday 15

_____

_____

EASTER SUNDAY Sunday 16

_____

_____

_____

FOR WE ARE GOD'S MASTERPIECE. HE HAS CREATED
US ANEW IN CHRIST JESUS, SO WE CAN DO THE
GOOD THINGS HE PLANNED FOR US LONG AGO.

Ephesians 2:10 NLT

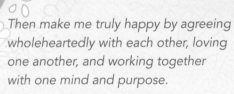

Then make me truly happy by agreeing wholeheartedly with each other, loving one another, and working together with one mind and purpose.

PHILIPPIANS 2:2 NLT

APRIL

17 Monday

_____
_____
_____
_____

18 Tuesday   LAST DAY OF PASSOVER

_____
_____
_____
_____

19 Wednesday

_____
_____
_____
_____

Thursday 20

Friday 21

Saturday 22

Sunday 23

BE OF THE SAME MIND TOWARD ONE ANOTHER. DO NOT
SET YOUR MIND ON HIGH THINGS, BUT ASSOCIATE WITH
THE HUMBLE. DO NOT BE WISE IN YOUR OWN OPINION.

Romans 12:16 NKJV

*Even when I walk through
the darkest valley,
I will not be afraid,
for you are close beside me.
Your rod and your staff protect
and comfort me.*

PSALM 23:4 NLT

APRIL

24 Monday

_____
_____
_____
_____

25 Tuesday

_____
_____
_____
_____
_____

26 Wednesday

_____
_____
_____
_____
_____

Thursday 27

_____

_____

_____

_____

_____

Friday 28

_____

_____

_____

_____

Saturday 29

_____

_____

_____

Sunday 30

_____

_____

_____

BE STRONG AND COURAGEOUS. DO NOT BE
FRIGHTENED, AND DO NOT BE DISMAYED, FOR THE
LORD YOUR GOD IS WITH YOU WHEREVER YOU GO.

Joshua 1:9 ESV

MAY
2017

Be my rock of refuge,

to which I can always go;

give the command to save me,

for you are my rock and my fortress….

You have been my hope, Sovereign LORD,

my confidence since my youth.

PSALM 71:3, 5 NIV

S	M	T	W	T	F	S
	1	2	3	4	5	6
7	8	9	10	11	12	13
14	15	16	17	18	19	20
21	22	23	24	25	26	27
28	29	30	31			

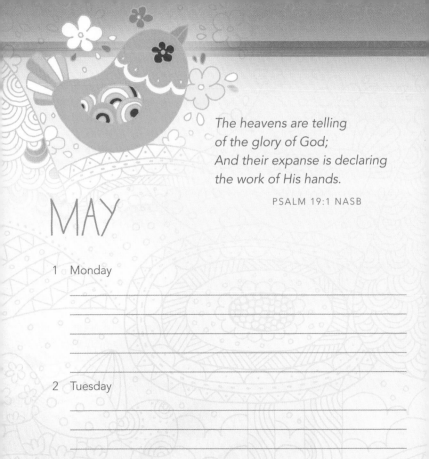

*The heavens are telling
of the glory of God;
And their expanse is declaring
the work of His hands.*

PSALM 19:1 NASB

MAY

1 Monday

2 Tuesday

3 Wednesday

Thursday 4

_____
_____
_____
_____
_____

Friday 5

_____
_____
_____
_____

Saturday 6

_____
_____
_____

Sunday 7

_____
_____
_____

THE WHOLE EARTH IS FILLED WITH AWE AT YOUR WONDERS.

Psalm 65:8 NIV

*The LORD hears his people
when they call to him for help.
He rescues them from all their troubles.*

PSALM 34:17 NLT

MAY

8   Monday

_____
_____
_____
_____

9   Tuesday

_____
_____
_____
_____

10 Wednesday

_____
_____
_____
_____

Thursday 11

_____

_____

_____

_____

Friday 12

_____

_____

_____

_____

Saturday 13

_____

_____

MOTHER'S DAY Sunday 14

_____

_____

_____

WHY AM I SO SAD?
WHY AM I SO UPSET?
I SHOULD PUT MY HOPE IN GOD
AND KEEP PRAISING HIM.

Psalm 42:11 NCV

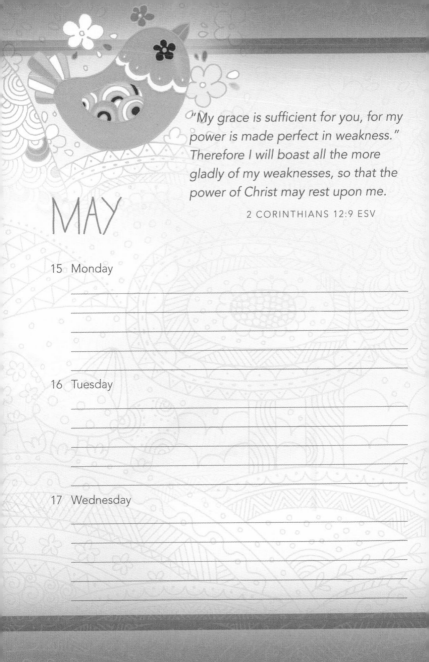

"My grace is sufficient for you, for my power is made perfect in weakness." Therefore I will boast all the more gladly of my weaknesses, so that the power of Christ may rest upon me.

2 CORINTHIANS 12:9 ESV

MAY

15 Monday

16 Tuesday

17 Wednesday

Thursday 18

Friday 19

Saturday 20

Sunday 21

Take a new grip with your tired hands and strengthen your weak knees. Mark out a straight path for your feet so that those who are weak and lame will not fall but become strong.

Hebrews 12:12-14 NLT

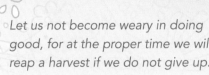

Let us not become weary in doing good, for at the proper time we will reap a harvest if we do not give up.

GALATIANS 6:9 NIV

MAY

22 Monday

_____
_____
_____
_____

23 Tuesday

_____
_____
_____
_____
_____

24 Wednesday

_____
_____
_____
_____

Thursday 25

Friday 26

Saturday 27

Sunday 28

Let us not neglect our meeting together, as some
people do, but encourage one another, especially
now that the day of his return is drawing near.

Hebrews 10:25 NLT

Let us not become weary in doing good, for at the proper time we will reap a harvest if we do not give up.

GALATIANS 6:9 NIV

MAY/JUNE

29 Monday   MEMORIAL DAY

_____
_____
_____
_____

30 Tuesday

_____
_____
_____
_____

31 Wednesday

_____
_____
_____
_____

Thursday 1

_____

_____

_____

_____

Friday 2

_____

_____

_____

_____

Saturday 3

_____

_____

PENTECOST Sunday 4

_____

_____

_____

LET US NOT NEGLECT OUR MEETING TOGETHER, AS SOME
PEOPLE DO, BUT ENCOURAGE ONE ANOTHER, ESPECIALLY
NOW THAT THE DAY OF HIS RETURN IS DRAWING NEAR.

Hebrews 10:25 NLT

JUNE
2017

The LORD your God is in your midst,

a mighty one who will save;

he will rejoice over you with gladness;

he will quiet you by his love;

he will exult over you with loud singing.

ZEPHANIAH 3:17 ESV

Dress clothes
Shoes - Black
Hygiene Items
Hair Bartletts

S	M	T	W	T	F	S
				1	2	3
4	5	6	7	8	9	10
11	12	13	14	15	16	17
18	19	20	21	22	23	24
25	26	27	28	29	30	

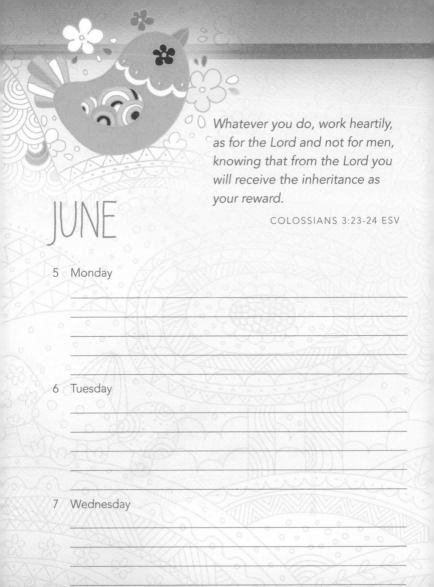

Whatever you do, work heartily, as for the Lord and not for men, knowing that from the Lord you will receive the inheritance as your reward.

COLOSSIANS 3:23-24 ESV

JUNE

5   Monday

6   Tuesday

7   Wednesday

Thursday 8

_____

_____

_____

_____

Friday 9

_____

_____

_____

_____

Saturday 10

_____

_____

Sunday 11

_____

_____

_____

Do your best to present yourself to God as one
approved by him, a worker who has no need to be
ashamed, rightly explaining the word of truth.

2 Timothy 2:15 NRSV

*Before the mountains
were brought forth,
or ever you had formed
the earth and the world,
from everlasting to
everlasting you are God.*

PSALM 90:2 ESV

JUNE

12 Monday

13 Tuesday

14 Wednesday FLAG DAY

Thursday 15

_____

_____

_____

_____

_____

Friday 16

_____

_____

_____

_____

_____

Saturday 17

_____

_____

_____

Sunday 18

_____

_____

_____

"I WILL COME BACK AND TAKE YOU TO BE WITH
ME THAT YOU ALSO MAY BE WHERE I AM."

John 14:3 NIV

His divine power has granted to us everything pertaining to life and godliness, through the true knowledge of Him who called us by His own glory and excellence.

2 PETER 1:3 NASB

JUNE

19 Monday

20 Tuesday

21 Wednesday   SUMMER SOLSTICE

_____

_____

_____

_____

_____

_____

_____

_____

_____

_____

_____

_____

_____

_____

_____

_____

"IF YOU HAVE FAITH LIKE A GRAIN OF MUSTARD SEED, YOU WILL SAY
TO THIS MOUNTAIN, 'MOVE FROM HERE TO THERE,' AND IT WILL
MOVE, AND NOTHING WILL BE IMPOSSIBLE FOR YOU."

Matthew 17:20 ESV

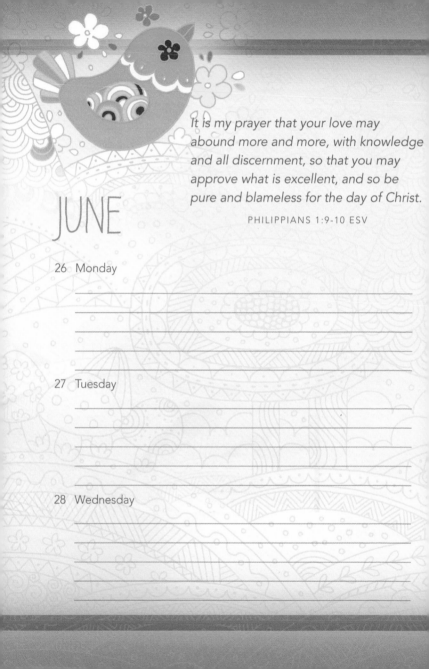

It is my prayer that your love may abound more and more, with knowledge and all discernment, so that you may approve what is excellent, and so be pure and blameless for the day of Christ.

PHILIPPIANS 1:9-10 ESV

JUNE

26 Monday

_____
_____
_____
_____

27 Tuesday

_____
_____
_____
_____

28 Wednesday

_____
_____
_____
_____

Thursday 29

Friday 30

Saturday 1

Sunday 2

THEREFORE, WHETHER YOU EAT OR DRINK,
OR WHATEVER YOU DO, DO ALL TO THE GLORY OF GOD.

1 Corinthians 10:31 NKJV

JULY
2017

For you created my inmost being;

you knit me together in my mother's womb.

I praise you because I am fearfully

and wonderfully made;

your works are wonderful,

I know that full well.

PSALM 139:13-14 NIV

S	M	T	W	T	F	S
						1
2	3	4	5	6	7	8
9	10	11	12	13	14	15
16	17	18	19	20	21	22
23	24	25	26	27	28	29
30	31					

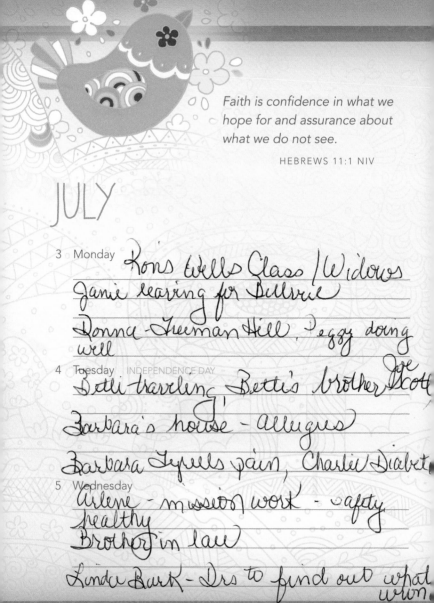

Faith is confidence in what we hope for and assurance about what we do not see.

HEBREWS 11:1 NIV

JULY

3 Monday

Ron's Wells Class / Widows

Jamie leaving for Bellevue

Donna - Freeman Hill, Peggy doing well

4 Tuesday INDEPENDENCE DAY

Betti traveling, Betti's brother Joe Scott

Barbara's house - Allergies

Barbara Tyrells pain, Charlie/Diabet

5 Wednesday

Arlene - mission work - safety healthy

Brother in law

Linda Bark - Drs to find out what wron

Susan, unspoken Kelly + Ryan - son

Jimmie - friend Kidney Cancer

Church - prayer and staff

WITHOUT FAITH IT IS IMPOSSIBLE TO PLEASE GOD, BECAUSE
ANYONE WHO COMES TO HIM MUST BELIEVE THAT HE EXISTS
AND THAT HE REWARDS THOSE WHO EARNESTLY SEEK HIM.

Hebrews 11:6 NIV

> For the word of the LORD is upright,
> and all his work is done in faithfulness.
>
> PSALM 33:4 ESV

Pg 124   past
          yourself
JULY   God & myself
          Redeem
          Pray - Praise

I Solomon
Center of your
thought Close
Fgit not
God's promis

10 Monday

Arms of Jesus
Full of God and Ourselves
Decrease He increases
He has forgiven & forgot

11 Tuesday

(1) Phil 3: 12-13
What can I learn about Go
                          Myself
Redeem / Recap
What did I succeed at and

12 Wednesday

return to Christ as praise
Lumped them at the go
Phil 3:8
Pull & Purge which land in the
arms of Jesus - God wants

Thursday 13

to carry our load
Isa 22.15 Shebna was all about
who Him, ego trip. God had him
replaced because of his ressurection
of tomb. Remembered as a

Friday 14

FOOl!

Isaiah 49: God will never forget
us

something
Closey that brings Hope

Saturday 15

Romans 5:

Ps: 7 Vs. 6 · What do I remember

Sunday 16

GOD IS FAITHFUL. HE WILL NOT ALLOW THE
TEMPTATION TO BE MORE THAN YOU CAN STAND.
WHEN YOU ARE TEMPTED, HE WILL SHOW YOU A WAY
OUT SO THAT YOU CAN ENDURE.

1 Corinthians 10:13 NLT

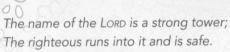

The name of the LORD is a strong tower;
The righteous runs into it and is safe.

PROVERBS 18:10 NASB

JULY

17 Monday

18 Tuesday

19 Wednesday

Thursday 20

_____

_____

_____

_____

Friday 21

_____

_____

_____

_____

Saturday 22

_____

_____

Sunday 23

_____

_____

_____

WHEN YOU LIE DOWN,
YOU WILL NOT BE AFRAID;
WHEN YOU LIE DOWN,
YOUR SLEEP WILL BE SWEET.

Proverbs 3:24 NIV

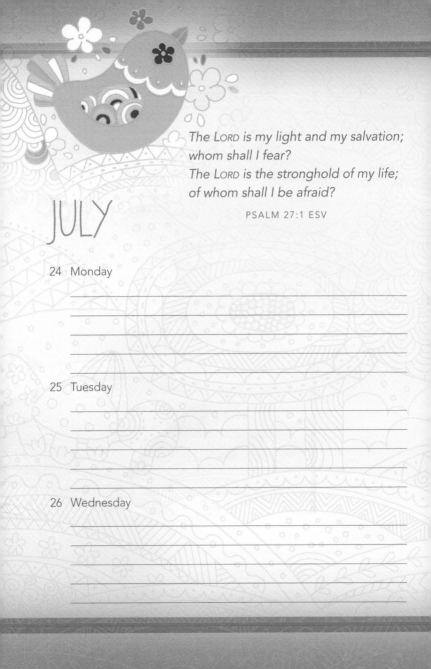

The LORD is my light and my salvation; whom shall I fear?
The LORD is the stronghold of my life; of whom shall I be afraid?

PSALM 27:1 ESV

JULY

24 Monday

25 Tuesday

26 Wednesday

Thursday 27

_____
_____
_____
_____
_____

Friday 28

_____
_____
_____
_____

Saturday 29

_____
_____
_____

Sunday 30

_____
_____
_____

FOR GOD HAS NOT GIVEN US A SPIRIT OF FEAR,
BUT OF POWER AND OF LOVE AND OF A SOUND MIND.

2 Timothy 1:7 NKJV

AUGUST
2017

Consider it pure joy, my brothers and sisters, whenever you face trials of many kinds, because you know that the testing of your faith produces perseverance.

JAMES 1:2-3 NIV

S	M	T	W	T	F	S
		1	2	3	4	5
6	7	8	9	10	11	12
13	14	15	16	17	18	19
20	21	22	23	24	25	26
27	28	29	30	31		

God is our refuge and strength, an ever-present help in trouble.

PSALM 46:1-3 NIV

JULY/AUGUST

31 Monday

_____

_____

_____

_____

1 Tuesday

_____

_____

_____

_____

2 Wednesday

_____

_____

_____

_____

_____

_____

_____

_____

_____

Friday   4

_____

_____

_____

_____

Saturday   5

_____

_____

_____

Sunday   6

_____

_____

_____

BUT NOW, O LORD,
YOU ARE OUR FATHER;
WE ARE THE CLAY, AND YOU OUR POTTER;
AND ALL WE ARE THE WORK OF YOUR HAND.

Isaiah 64:8 NKJV

If we confess our sins to him, he is faithful and just to forgive us our sins and to cleanse us from all wickedness.

1 JOHN 1:9 NLT

AUGUST

7   Monday

8   Tuesday

9   Wednesday

Thursday 10

_____

_____

_____

_____

_____

Friday 11

_____

_____

_____

_____

Saturday 12

_____

_____

_____

Sunday 13

_____

_____

_____

HE IS SO RICH IN KINDNESS AND GRACE THAT
HE PURCHASED OUR FREEDOM WITH THE
BLOOD OF HIS SON AND FORGAVE OUR SINS.

Ephesians 1:7 NLT

My sacrifice, O God,
is a broken spirit;
a broken and contrite heart you,
God, will not despise.

PSALM 51:17 NIV

AUGUST

14 Monday

15 Tuesday

16 Wednesday

Thursday 17

_____

_____

_____

_____

Friday 18

_____

_____

_____

_____

Saturday 19

_____

_____

Sunday 20

_____

_____

_____

For You, Lord, are good, and ready to forgive,
And abundant in mercy to all those who call upon You.

Psalm 86:5 NKJV

*It is more blessed
to give than to receive.*

ACTS 20:35 NIV

AUGUST

21 Monday

_____
_____
_____
_____

22 Tuesday

_____
_____
_____
_____

23 Wednesday

_____
_____
_____
_____

Thursday 24

Friday 25

Saturday 26

Sunday 27

WHOEVER IS GENEROUS TO THE POOR LENDS TO THE LORD,
AND HE WILL REPAY HIM FOR HIS DEED.

Proverbs 19:17 ESV

"Take my yoke upon you, and learn from me, for I am gentle and lowly in heart, and you will find rest your souls."

MATTHEW 11:29-30 ESV

AUGUST/SEPTEMBER

28 Monday

_____
_____
_____
_____

29 Tuesday

_____
_____
_____
_____

30 Wednesday

_____
_____
_____
_____

Thursday 31

_____
_____
_____
_____

Friday 1

_____
_____
_____
_____

Saturday 2

_____
_____

Sunday 3

_____
_____
_____

BLESSED ARE THE GENTLE, FOR THEY SHALL INHERIT THE EARTH.

Matthew 5:5 NASB

SEPTEMBER
2017

Therefore we do not lose heart, but though our outer man is decaying, yet our inner man is being renewed day by day. For momentary, light affliction is producing for us an eternal weight of glory far beyond all comparison.

2 CORINTHIANS 4:16-17 NASB

S	M	T	W	T	F	S
					1	2
3	4	5	6	7	8	9
10	11	12	13	14	15	16
17	18	19	20	21	22	23
24	25	26	27	28	29	30

*Taste and see that
the LORD is good;
blessed is the one
who takes refuge in him.*

PSALM 34:8 NIV

SEPTEMBER

4 Monday LABOR DAY

_____
_____
_____
_____

5 Tuesday

_____
_____
_____
_____

6 Wednesday

_____
_____
_____
_____

Thursday 7

_____

_____

_____

_____

_____

Friday 8

_____

_____

_____

_____

_____

Saturday 9

_____

_____

_____

Sunday 10

_____

_____

_____

THE LORD IS GOOD TO ALL,
AND HIS MERCY IS OVER ALL THAT HE HAS MADE.

Psalm 145:9 ESV

He will once again fill your mouth with laughter and your lips with shouts of joy.

JOB 8:21 NLT

SEPTEMBER

11 Monday

_____
_____
_____
_____

12 Tuesday

_____
_____
_____
_____

13 Wednesday

_____
_____
_____
_____

Thursday 14

_____

_____

_____

_____

Friday 15

_____

_____

_____

_____

Saturday 16

_____

_____

_____

Sunday 17

_____

_____

_____

THE RANSOMED OF THE LORD WILL RETURN. THEY WILL
ENTER ZION WITH SINGING; EVERLASTING JOY WILL CROWN
THEIR HEADS. GLADNESS AND JOY WILL OVERTAKE THEM,
AND SORROW AND SIGHING WILL FLEE AWAY.

Isaiah 35:10 NIV

To all who mourn in Israel he will give: beauty for ashes; joy instead of mourning; praise instead of heaviness. For God has planted them like strong and graceful oaks for his own glory.

ISAIAH 61:3 TLB

SEPTEMBER

18 Monday

_____
_____
_____
_____

19 Tuesday

_____
_____
_____
_____

20 Wednesday   ROSH HASHANAH BEGINS

_____
_____
_____
_____

Thursday 21

AUTUMNAL EQUINOX Friday 22

Saturday 23

Sunday 24

I CONSIDER THAT THE SUFFERINGS OF THIS PRESENT TIME ARE NOT
WORTH COMPARING WITH THE GLORY THAT IS TO BE REVEALED TO US.

Romans 8:18 ESV

Listen to advice and accept discipline, and at the end you will be counted among the wise.

PROVERBS 19:20 NIV

SEPTEMBER

25 Monday

26 Tuesday

27 Wednesday

Thursday 28

YOM KIPPUR BEGINS Friday 29

YOM KIPPUR ENDS Saturday 30

Sunday 1

WE CAN MAKE OUR PLANS, BUT THE LORD DETERMINES OUR STEPS.

Proverbs 16:9 NLT

OCTOBER
2017

With me are riches and honor,

enduring wealth and prosperity.

My fruit is better than fine gold;

what I yield surpasses choice silver.

I walk in the way of righteousness,

along the paths of justice,

bestowing a rich inheritance

on those who love me

and making their treasuries full.

PROVERBS 8:18-21 NIV

S	M	T	W	T	F	S
1	2	3	4	5	6	7
8	9	10	11	12	13	14
15	16	17	18	19	20	21
22	23	24	25	26	27	28
29	30	31				

"Nothing is hidden that will not be made manifest, nor is anything secret that will not be known and come to light."

LUKE 8:17 ESV

OCTOBER

2 Monday

_____
_____
_____
_____

3 Tuesday

_____
_____
_____
_____
_____

4 Wednesday

_____
_____
_____
_____

Thursday 5

_____

_____

_____

_____

Friday 6

_____

_____

_____

_____

Saturday 7

_____

_____

Sunday 8

_____

_____

_____

THOSE WHO DEAL TRUTHFULLY ARE HIS DELIGHT.

Proverbs 12:22 NKJV

Whoever pursues righteousness and love finds life, prosperity and honor.

PROVERBS 21:21 NIV

OCTOBER

9 **Monday**   COLUMBUS DAY

_____

_____

_____

_____

10 **Tuesday**

_____

_____

_____

_____

11 **Wednesday**

_____

_____

_____

_____

_____
_____
_____
_____
_____

_____
_____
_____
_____
_____

_____
_____
_____

_____
_____
_____

"MY FATHER WILL HONOR THE ONE WHO SERVES ME."

John 12:26 NIV

May the God of hope fill you with all joy and peace as you trust in him, so that you may overflow with hope by the power of the Holy Spirit.

ROMANS 15:13 NIV

OCTOBER

16 Monday

_____
_____
_____
_____
_____

17 Tuesday

_____
_____
_____
_____
_____

18 Wednesday

_____
_____
_____
_____
_____

Thursday 19

Friday 20

Saturday 21

Sunday 22

THE LORD TAKES PLEASURE IN THOSE WHO FEAR HIM,
IN THOSE WHO HOPE IN HIS MERCY.

Psalm 147:11 NKJV

*The LORD has told you what is good,
and this is what he requires of you:
to do what is right, to love mercy,
and to walk humbly with your God.*

MICAH 6:8 NLT

OCTOBER

23 Monday

_____
_____
_____
_____

24 Tuesday

_____
_____
_____
_____

25 Wednesday

_____
_____
_____
_____

Thursday 26

Friday 27

Saturday 28

Sunday 29

Pride will ruin people,
but those who are humble will be honored.

Proverbs 29:23 NCV

NOVEMBER
2017

My child, pay attention to what I say.

Listen carefully to my words.

Don't lose sight of them.

Let them penetrate deep into your heart,

for they bring life to those who find them,

and healing to their whole body.

PROVERBS 4:20-22 NLT

S	M	T	W	T	F	S
			1	2	3	4
5	6	7	8	9	10	11
12	13	14	15	16	17	18
19	20	21	22	23	24	25
26	27	28	29	30		

*The precepts of
the LORD are right,
giving joy to the heart.
The commands of
the LORD are radiant,
giving light to the eyes.*

PSALM 19:8 NIV

OCTOBER/NOVEMBER

30 Monday

_____

_____

_____

_____

_____

31 Tuesday

_____

_____

_____

_____

_____

1 Wednesday

_____

_____

_____

_____

Thursday 2

_____

_____

_____

_____

Friday 3

_____

_____

_____

_____

Saturday 4

_____

_____

_____

DAYLIGHT SAVING TIME ENDS Sunday 5

_____

_____

_____

YOUR LAWS ARE MY TREASURE;
THEY ARE MY HEART'S DELIGHT.

Psalm 119:111 NLT

People with integrity walk safely, but those who follow crooked paths will slip and fall.

PROVERBS 10:9 NLT

NOVEMBER

Shultz
John + Ginger - Dee Me
staff infection Chism
Sherry - Praise
& Steve

6 Monday

Carrie Mitchell

Alicia

Donna

Dar church

Cheryl Maler / Earl fell

7 Tuesday ELECTION DAY

Cindy Snidow

Linda Pile - rash. 2 weeks
doing better, what is causing
Dizzyness

8 Wednesday

Jacob, Dad - Salvation brother-in-law

Chuck job - Mark Roberts lung
56 Cancer

Charlee - tummy

Barbara - itching - nerves

Jennie 6.months

Heart - family

Susans throat

Linda - mastectomy

Kelly + Michael possible moving
acting like brats

Sandra - Amy relationship; grandkids

BECAUSE OF MY INTEGRITY YOU UPHOLD ME
AND SET ME IN YOUR PRESENCE FOREVER.

Psalm 41:12 NIV

"These things I have spoken to you, that My joy may remain in you, and that your joy may be full."

JOHN 15:11 NKJV

NOVEMBER

13 Monday

_____
_____
_____
_____

14 Tuesday

_____
_____
_____
_____

15 Wednesday

_____
_____
_____
_____

Thursday 16

_____

_____

_____

_____

_____

Friday 17

_____

_____

_____

_____

_____

Saturday 18

_____

_____

_____

Sunday 19

_____

_____

_____

YOU WILL GO OUT WITH JOY AND BE LED OUT IN PEACE.
THE MOUNTAINS AND HILLS WILL BURST INTO SONG BEFORE YOU,
AND ALL THE TREES IN THE FIELDS WILL CLAP THEIR HANDS.

Isaiah 55:12 NCV

The LORD secures justice for the poor and upholds the cause of the needy.

PSALM 140:12 NIV

NOVEMBER

20 Monday

_____
_____
_____
_____

21 Tuesday

_____
_____
_____
_____

22 Wednesday

_____
_____
_____
_____

_____
_____
_____
_____
_____

Friday 24

_____
_____
_____
_____
_____

Saturday 25

_____
_____
_____

Sunday 26

_____
_____
_____

RIGHTEOUSNESS AND JUSTICE ARE
THE FOUNDATION OF YOUR THRONE.

Psalm 89:14 NIV

*"Look, I am coming soon!
My reward is with me, and I will
give to each person according
to what they have done."*

REV 22:12 NIV

NOVEMBER/DECEMBER

27 Monday

_____
_____
_____
_____

28 Tuesday

_____
_____
_____
_____

29 Wednesday

_____
_____
_____
_____

Thursday 30

_____

_____

_____

_____

_____

Friday 1

_____

_____

_____

_____

_____

Saturday 2

_____

_____

_____

FIRST SUNDAY OF ADVENT   Sunday 3

_____

_____

_____

THE LORD IS COMING TO JUDGE THE EARTH.
HE WILL JUDGE THE WORLD WITH JUSTICE,
AND THE NATIONS WITH FAIRNESS.

Psalm 98:9 NLT

DECEMBER
2017

"You are the light of the world. A city set on a hill cannot be hidden. Nor do people light a lamp and put it under a basket, but on a stand, and it gives light to all in the house. In the same way, let your light shine before others, so that they may see your good works and give glory to your Father who is in heaven."

MATTHEW 5:14-16 ESV

S	M	T	W	T	F	S
					1	2
3	4	5	6	7	8	9
10	11	12	13	14	15	16
17	18	19	20	21	22	23
24	25	26	27	28	29	30
31						

*His merciful kindness
is great toward us,
And the truth of the Lord
endures forever.*

PSALM 117:2 NKJV

DECEMBER

4 Monday

_____
_____
_____
_____

5 Tuesday

_____
_____
_____
_____

6 Wednesday

_____
_____
_____
_____

Thursday 7

Friday 8

Saturday 9

Sunday 10

"LOVE YOUR ENEMIES, AND DO GOOD, AND LEND, EXPECTING
NOTHING IN RETURN, AND YOUR REWARD WILL BE GREAT,
AND YOU WILL BE SONS OF THE MOST HIGH."

Luke 6:35 ESV

"Come to me,
all you who are weary
and burdened,
and I will give you rest."

MATTHEW 11:28 NIV

DECEMBER

11 Monday

_____
_____
_____
_____
_____

12 Tuesday   HANUKKAH BEGINS

_____
_____
_____
_____

13 Wednesday

_____
_____
_____
_____
_____

Thursday 14

Friday 15

Saturday 16

Sunday 17

Satisfy us in the morning with your unfailing love,
that we may sing for joy and be glad all our days.

Psalm 90:14 NIV

Three things will last forever—
faith, hope, and love—
and the greatest of these is love.

1 CORINTHIANS 13:13 NLT

DECEMBER

18 Monday

_____
_____
_____
_____
_____

19 Tuesday

_____
_____
_____
_____
_____

20 Wednesday HANUKKAH ENDS

_____
_____
_____
_____
_____

Friday 22

Saturday 23

THEY WHO WAIT FOR THE LORD SHALL RENEW THEIR
STRENGTH; THEY SHALL MOUNT UP WITH WINGS LIKE EAGLES;
THEY SHALL RUN AND NOT BE WEARY;
THEY SHALL WALK AND NOT FAINT.

Isaiah 40:31 ESV

Be like those who through faith and patience will receive what God has promised.

HEBREWS 6:12 NCV

DECEMBER

25 **Monday** CHRISTMAS DAY

_____
_____
_____
_____

26 Tuesday

_____
_____
_____
_____

27 Wednesday

_____
_____
_____
_____

Thursday 28

Friday 29

Saturday 30

NEW YEAR'S EVE Sunday 31

I WAIT FOR THE LORD, MY WHOLE BEING WAITS,
AND IN HIS WORD I PUT MY HOPE.

Psalm 130:5 NIV

Belle City Gifts
Racine, Wisconsin, USA

Belle City Gifts is an imprint of BroadStreet Publishing Group LLC.
Broadstreetpublishing.com

A Little God Time 2017 Planner
© 2016 by BroadStreet Publishing

ISBN 978-1-4245-5274-0

Design by Garborg Design Works | www.garborgdesign.com
Compiled and edited by Michelle Winger | www.literallyprecise.com

Printed in China.

16 17 18 19 20 21 22   7 6 5 4 3 2 1

Insurance

Tulips
Daffodils
Allium

Linda Pate 4-1-48 (4)
Jimmie Lamar 11/16 (9)
Susan Carter 1-8-51 (1)
Betti Owens 7-18-38 (8)
Jenni Parsons 1-14-41 (2)
Robbie Craddock 7-29-49 (7)
Donna Grice 3-29-42 (3)
Barbara Thompson 7/1/51 (6)(5)
Sandra Blackard 5-13-48